A
SPORTS
BESTIARY

Other books by George Plimpton:

Out of My League
Paper Lion
The Bogey Man
Mad Ducks and Bears
One for the Record
One More July
Shadow Box
American Journey: The Times of Robert F. Kennedy (with Jean Stein)
Edie: An American Biography (with Jean Stein)
Writers at Work: Five Volumes (editor)

Other books enhanced by Arnold Roth:

Houseful of Laughter by Bennett Cerf
Grimm's Fairy Tales
What Every Nice Boy Knew About Sex by Samuel Blum
I Hear America Mating by Ralph Schoenstein
The President's Mystery Plot by F. D. Roosevelt
East vs. West by Ralph Schoenstein
The Hater's Handbook by Joseph Rosner

A SPORTS BESTIARY

by George Plimpton

With drawings
by Arnold Roth

McGRAW-HILL BOOK COMPANY

New York   St. Louis   San Francisco   Toronto   Mexico

1 2 3 4 5 6 7 8 9 DOW DOW 8 7 6 5 4 3 2

ISBN 0-07-050290-0

Library of Congress Cataloging in Publication Data

Plimpton, George.
A sports bestiary.
1. Sports—Anecdotes, facetiae, satire, etc.
I. Roth, Arnold, 1929-   . II. Title.
PN6231.S65P5 1982   818′.5402   82-10002
ISBN 0-07-050290-0   AACR2

Book design by Stanley S. Drate

For Medora and Taylor
G. A. P.

For Richard Gangel, Frank Zachary, and Jerome Alten
A. R.

CONTENTS

INTRODUCTION

This book is not actually a bestiary. It is what most people *think* a bestiary is—namely an assemblage of vividly imagined beasts who behave somewhat quirkily, bear only the vaguest application to real life, and are known mostly as heraldic fixtures. In fact, the animals of a true medieval bestiary (the griffin, the cameleopard, the unicorn, and so forth), although they would seem to be the products of lively flights of fancy, in fact are the result of serious scientific work. At least it was the best that the authorities of those times could do.

Physiologus is generally thought to have written the first bestiary, probably in Greek, at some time between the second and fifth centuries. Entitled *Physiologus* (how handy to be both author and title of your book!), the ancient treatise discussed a total of forty-nine beasts, starting with the lion. Physiologus had probably never seen a lion, much less observed its behavior in the wild, so he was simply reporting what he believed when he wrote that a lion cub was born dead and brought to life when the male lion passed by in three days and breathed in its face. Or that a bear's offspring was born a shapeless lump and was licked and molded into recognizable ursine shape by its mother's tongue. That was as common knowledge in those times as it is today in the Kentucky hills that hoop snakes put their tails in their mouths and roll down the slopes like runaway bicycle tires.

There is one essential difference between the animals of the ancient bestiaries and such creatures of backwoods lore as the hoop snake—which is that invariably moral lessons and sermons were drawn from the former. For example, Physiologus describes the whale as a figure of the devil, as large as an island, to which unknowing sailors would tie their ships and start lighting cooking fires. The whale, feeling the heat on its skin, "urinates and plunges into the depths, sinking all the ships." Then the author goes on to pontificate, "You also, O man, if you fix and bind yourself to the hope of the devil, he will plunge you along with himself into hell-fire." The meaning of such symbolism was so significant to the medieval mind that the importance of the animal—this according to St. Augustine—was not that it existed but what it *meant*.

In the *Sports Bestiary*—we hope not to the reader's woe—there is no attempt to emulate Physiologus. The Suicide Squeeze has not been lifted from an instruction booklet on baseball with attendant warnings on its proper use ("You also, O manager, if you fix and bind yourself to the Suicide Squeeze, he will plunge you . . ."). The reader, of course, is free to draw conclusions from the text, but the authors would support the kind of admonition Mark Twain gives the readers of *Huckleberry Finn,* that "persons attempting to find a moral . . . will be banished."

There is a great deal about sex in the medieval bestiaries. For example, the viper, which is much more lustful according to the ancient texts than I ever knew, is not content to enjoy the company of other vipers; it tries to seduce eels, which it calls out of the sea with a wolf whistle.

Once again, we have not concentrated on this aspect with our creatures. Mr. Roth, who is uncomfortable drawing such scenes, having been raised in Philadelphia, asked me at the outset to keep such disclosures to a minimum. Thus, I believe only the mating habits of those strange beasts the Ump and the End Zone are described.

The point of departure for almost all the creatures in this bestiary has been the nomenclature of sport. There is very little in the sports lexicon that does not bring a creature, often a monster, to mind. A small child breaks into tears when his father informs him at breakfast that he will not be home for dinner that evening because he is going to see a Twi-Night Doubleheader. What an awesome figure looms in the youngster's imagination! Sports has a plethora of such terms that beg for bestiarizing. To think that Mr. Roth and I have not tackled the Tight End, or the Break Point, or even the Half-Volley! They continue to stalk around out there unmolested.

A
SPORTS
BESTIARY

THE RAW TALENT

An ostrichlike bird who has taken it into his head that he can play striker for the New York Cosmos. He is not a half-bad soccer player, though he has a tendency to run out of the stadium and get mixed up out among the cars in the parking lots. On the playing field, he is admired for his speed, his height (he is twice as tall as any of the other players), and a backward kick that is devastating if the ball (or for that matter an opponent) happens to be in its path. True, he is not very good at heading the ball—his comparatively tiny head has on occasion been dislocated by coming in contact with the larger and heavier soccer ball—and he has a disconcerting habit of sitting on the soccer ball and trying to hatch it. But just about every coach in the league believes the Raw Talent can be developed.

3

THE MOMENTUM

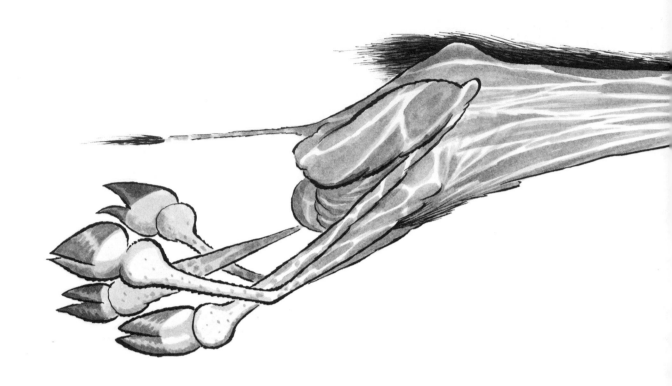

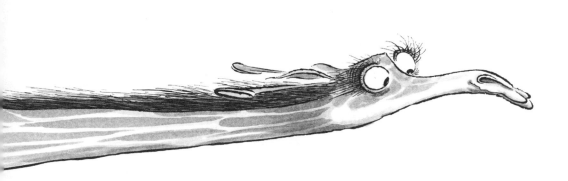

A somewhat charming okapi that on occasion tilts forward to browse on the top of a bush and, off balance, is carried forward by his own weight, sometimes for a considerable headlong distance, until he fetches up against a foreign object, usually a hippogriff. The curiously appealing, and much sought-after, beast is also done in by Overconfidence, Lack of Talent, a Serious Injury, Behemoths on the Other Team, George Steinbrenner, III, loss of the equipment trunks, No Soap in the Shower Stalls, the End of the Season, and especially by No Money in the Till. Once lost, the Momentum hibernates, especially in Toronto.

THE END ZONE

End Zones are extremely flat, rectangular-shaped members of the tortoise family. These carpetlike creatures come in pairs. They do not enjoy each other's company, apparently, since they always stay exactly one hundred yards apart; in Canada, they seem to be even less sociable, staying one hundred and ten yards from each other. No one has ever seen an End Zone mate, though they must do it somehow, perhaps very late at night, because there are an awful lot of them. Sometimes people wearing cleats run onto the backs of End Zones and throw down a spheroid very hard. Called spiking, this process may be an artificial method of inseminating an End Zone. Certainly a lot of cheering goes up when it happens. Sometimes an End Zone, as is the custom with turtles, gets his back painted with big lettering—ARKANSAS or GIANTS. The End Zone does not seem to mind. He is an extremely somnambulant and easygoing sort.

THE CLIFFHANGER

A flightless ducklike bird that hangs from precipices by its beak—a sight that tends to produce consternation and hand-wringing in those who happen to come around a bend and see it. Cliffhangers stay in the mind longer than others of the species such as the Rout, the Breezer, the Ho-Hum, and the Laugher—ducks that stand around and do little more than molt. Not the Cliffhanger. This bird's odd habit causes finger-biting and head-clutching, and can produce ulcers, especially when one sees four or five in a row.

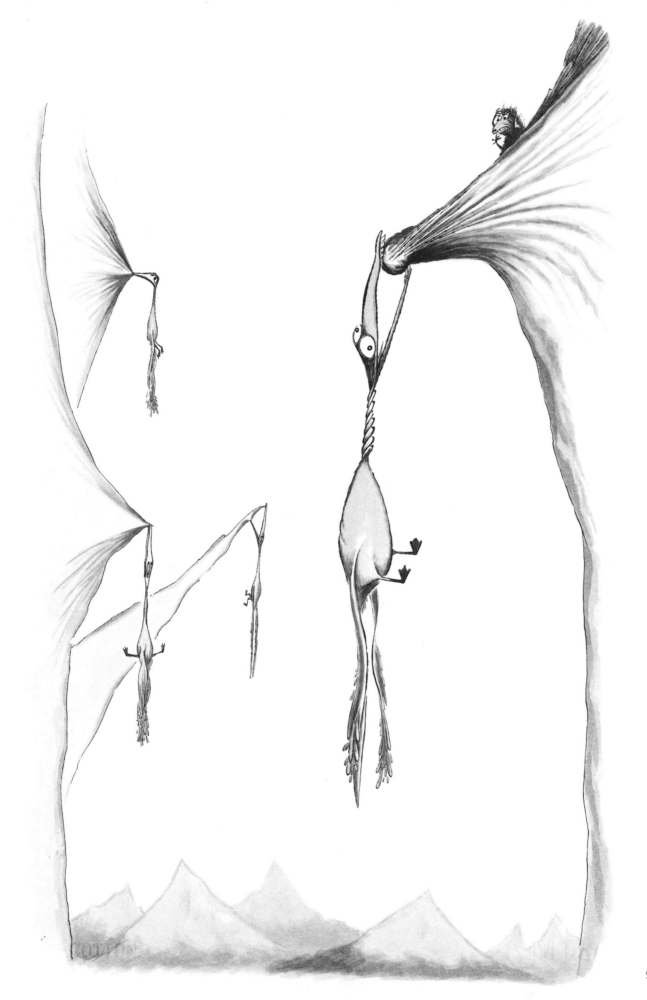

THE SOLID LEFT HOOK

A relative of the common Jab family known to anyone who keeps a fish tank. But unlike those quick little flickering fellows dodging in and out of their alabaster castles, the Solid Left Hook is an amazingly boring goldfish that simply stares through the fishbowl glass and fills the vision. It is the sort of gift one would rather give than receive. Occasionally, a small oily bubble emerges from its mouth, which makes the viewer feel quite woozy. There is a variety of Hook, a very leathery sort, known as the Whistling Left Hook (although no one has actually ever heard it), which may be a better gift, but anyone who receives a Solid Left Hook as a pet is really in for it. Two or three Solid Left Hooks are much worse than one—especially three in a row, staring through the fishbowl glass and working up those oily bubbles in their respective gullets. That is enough to stagger any pet owner.

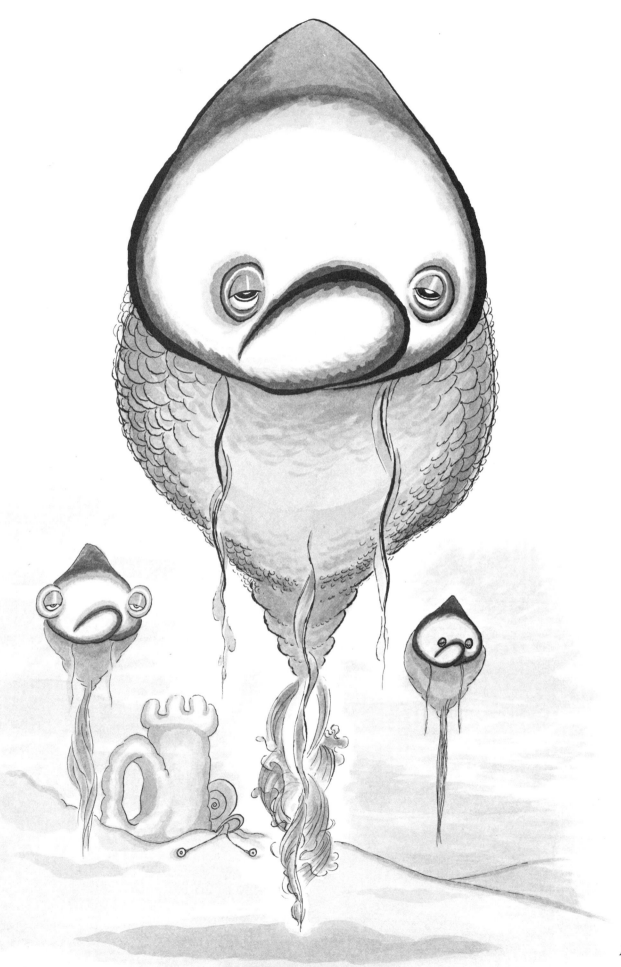

THE HANGING CURVE

A cheerful, fastidious, plump, and somewhat curvaceous member of the partridge family who tends to get eaten a lot. As every gourmet knows, the Hanging Curve is prepared for the table in a variety of ways: "pickled"; "smoked"; "creamed"; "made mincemeat of"; "pasted." Even before he reaches the pot, the Hanging Curve seems to bring out voraciousness in just about everyone. He gets "pummeled"; "pole-axed"; "leaned into"; "jumped on"; "hammered"; "walloped"; "blasted"; "crucified." He is also known to have been "rolled to the wall." Some people have the curious habit of "throwing" the Hanging Curve. Those who do so invariably get under such a fallout of fluff and feathers that they are forced to take showers. In fact, the Hanging Curve is famous for sending people to the showers.

"Why did Rogers go to the showers?"

"The Hanging Curve."

"Oh."

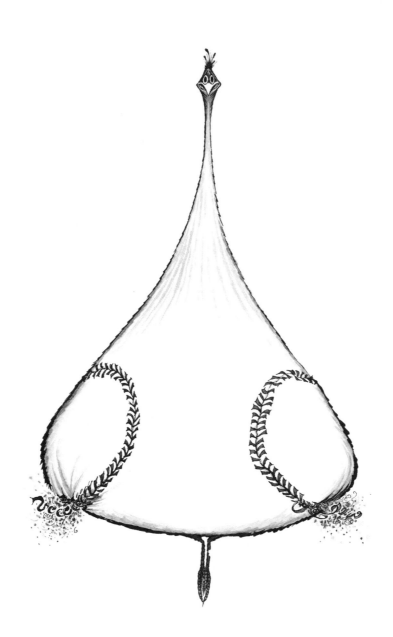

THE LOB

A rather feeble, fat, fuzz-covered, rotund insect, usually entirely white, but often green, yellow, or even orange, that believes he can achieve a height that will put him into orbit around the earth. The Lob suffers a severe case of delusions of grandeur. He rarely rises more than thirty feet. He gets whacked with a large flyswatter more than he would like to, and gets "put away."

Except for this odd desire to achieve orbit, the Lob is a rather traditional sort. He incubates, invariably in the company of two others of his kind, in a dark, cylinderlike cocoon, often for years at a time. Eventually, though, he emerges—with a loud, hissing gasp of annoyance and a belch, remarkable for an insect so rotund, that leaves a strong rubbery smell in the vicinity. He then goes about the usual activity of normal flies—zipping here and there—until this infernal notion of trying to get into orbit comes to mind. The shortish Lobs have a terrible time of it and invariably get put away.

THE SIS-BOOM-BAH

The Sis-Boom-Bah is one of a large family of flying foxes that live in the throats of megaphones and tend to emerge on weekend afternoons. Some people are said to be inspired by the sight of these animals; they sit on hillsides and call out their names in great thunderous choruses as they appear. The most common of the species is the Rah. The Sooo-eee (an Arkansas subspecies) and the Hook 'm Horns (from Texas) are melanistic phases. The Hold-That-Line and the *Dee*-fense are both as common as starlings. Very rare is the Fight Fiercely, a Cambridge, Massachusetts, subspecies known for his timidity; on occasion he topples from the lip of the megaphone and falls to the ground. The family is an ancient one. Fossilized remains of the Sis-Boom-Bah have been found in Greece, an early ancestor known as the Brekekekex, ko-ax, ko-ax.

17

THE REVERSE LAYUP

A very agitated, rubbery-bodied canine who looks a lot like an elongated Afghan. He leaps up a lot and gets caught on wall fixtures and chandeliers. The species wears the slightly pained, hopeful look of one who hopes to please, but who cannot do the simplest act without complicating things. No sooner does he move forward to retrieve a slipper for his master than he suddenly reverses himself and backs into the fireplace. He is prone to fetching the newspaper from the front walk and putting it in the fire. One might suppose that the simple act of lying down might be easy for the Reverse Layup. Not at all. As his name implies, he revolves, he twists; perhaps he will sleep standing up. Nonetheless, he is an appealing pet. He can be missed. A groan goes up when he is missed. One wonders why. Perhaps people enjoy seeing an easy thing made difficult, and that is what the Reverse Layup seems to do.

THE UMP

The Ump is a large, rubbery-looking guinea fowl. Usually four of them appear within the borders of a field. They stand apart from each other, lonely figures in a Magritte landscape. The plumage of the Ump is black. The Ump's feet are stout and heavy. He shows his displeasure by turning his back on those who torment him. The worst thing that can happen to an Ump is to have dust kicked on his feet, or to have handfuls of dirt thrown at him. Whoever is responsible is immediately given the Thumb (cf) by the Ump, who has a number of these quasi-gifts on hand. Authorities continue to be puzzled by the activities of the Umps on the field. It is thought that the four of them are involved in some kind of mating ritual. One of the Umps, usually the largest and most rubbery-looking, squats down as if to lay an egg, and then *does not*. He rises. He squats. Sometimes he becomes quite agitated and delivers a long, drawn-out cry, "Steeee-a-rike!" often pointing a wing off to one side as he does. He then looks around to see if an impression has been made on any of the other Umps. Usually none has. They look off in different directions. Sometimes one of the other Umps will run a short distance and call out, "Fowl!" None of the other Umps is interested. No one has ever seen an Ump mate on the field, though it is presumed that they must do it somewhere since there are a lot of them around, especially in the summer.

THE THUMB

A small black-thumbed parrot with milky eyes that in his wicker cage is often given as a gift often by an Ump (cf). He is not a popular gift at all. No one likes to be given the Thumb. He turns out not to talk; he makes gestures with his claws that are meaningful but not pleasant. The Thumb tends to let loose with a great outcry in the early hours of the morning. He likes the taste of wicker and slowly consumes his own cage. To have him loose in the house is a good enough reason to pack the suitcases and move to a hotel. The Thumb has a number of close relatives—the Boot, the Deep Six, the Shaft, the Ax, the Gate, and the Finger. All are disagreeable pets and no one wants to get any of them—especially the Finger.

THE HI MOM

A cheerful, somewhat homely bat, with a large sweat-stained face, who hangs upside down on television cameras, peers into the lens, and says as follows: "Hi Mom!" Often he does not say it aloud; he mouths it. Hence his name. The Hi Mom picks very curious times to heave suddenly into view—usually in the middle of postfight interviews with boxing champions being conducted by Howard Cosell in mid-ring. Just as Mr. Cosell intones: "As evidenced by the severe contusion on your—" the Hi Mom appears, obscuring the TV screen with his smiling bat's visage. "Hi Mom!" he says. Sometimes he is accompanied by a rarer species, the Hi Sis, and on extremely rare occasions by the Hi-Bobby-Gottlieb-and-All-the-Gang-Down-at-Alfred's. The Hi Mom is not to be confused with the We're Number Ones, who are a large species of sea lion and sit in tierlike rows on their rocks, pointing their flippers to the heavens. Howard Cosell, who is a sportscaster, does not approve of any of these species. He tries to fill the TV screen with his own visage. But he does not say anything like "Hi Mom!"

THE CLUBHOUSE TURN

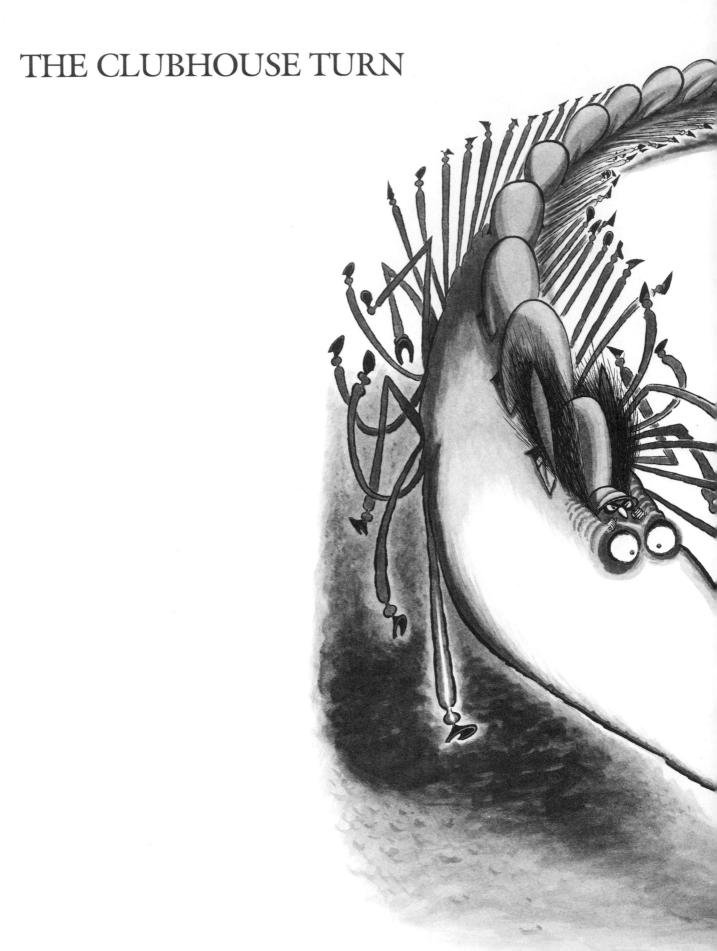

A millipedelike creature that hangs around wide dirt roads and often comes around the corner running sideways, so that one sees a multitude of feet or paws or hooves (it's difficult to tell) approaching at a considerable clip. Seen through binoculars, he has two tiers of eyes—the ones on top small and nasty, the lower ones large with the whites showing from fear. The Clubhouse Turn comes in on a tear eight times a day. Sometimes observers are happy at what they see coming toward them and they leap up and down and carry on; sometimes, though, they are not happy at all: they shout at the Clubhouse Turn, "Ah, you couldn't beat my grandmother!" He is a very confusing animal and I do not want to write any more about him. Go out and see the Turn for yourself if you must.

THE JIBE

There are two species of Jibe—the Intentional and the Unintentional. Both in conformation look very much alike—great pterodactyl-like birds with stiff, triangular wings, often with a red "14" in the corner. Their habit is to skim the surface of the seas, tilting in the wind currents. The Intentional is mild-mannered and in control of himself. He can turn around the lea of a lighthouse with great éclat and a minimum of fuss. On the other hand, the Unintentional is haphazard, unpredictable; he often catches a wing tip and capsizes into the sea, or a nun, and has been known to clear an entire deckload of Nantucket vacationers with a scything pass close aboard. The sudden approach of an Unintentional Jibe is often heralded by a lot of people calling out "Uh-oh!" and "Look out!" and a scrambling to duck before the Unintentional blots out the sun.

THE DRIBBLE

A low-slung camel with a half hump that lurches across the terrain in little fits and starts. He looks haunted. His terror is that he will be interrupted. When he moves across wood he cries out rhythmically *thonk thonk thonk*. Across the grass he is silent. He is a good, if somewhat large and erratic, pet. He keeps to the vicinity of one's heels. He darts off in little scampering runs. Only the Tackle (cf) disturbs the tenor of the Dribble's day. Sir Stanley Matthews, Pele, and Giorgio Chinaglia have fine Dribbles. No one knows the derivation of his name since the Dribble is usually dry-mouthed. He does not cost much to feed. In fact, no one knows what a Dribble eats.

THE TACKLE

A very large, obnoxious, destructive family of carnivores, very likely of the big cat or mouse variety, with the worst features of both (a mouse's tail and a cat's breath). Among the different subspecies of this large and disagreeable family are the Offensive, the Defensive, the Sure, the Flying, the Shoestring, the Gang, the Bone-Jarring, the Open-Field, the Teeth-Rattling, not to forget the Crushing and the Missed. All members of the Tackle family have a tendency to make things fall down. They are like houseguests who decimate an apartment as they move through; when they hang up the telephone it breaks in the cradle. The Tackle is especially hard on the Dribble (cf), the Broken-Field Runner, and the Tight End. There are those who are able to avoid or "break" the destructive pattern of the average Tackle, but then along comes another Tackle, usually the dreaded Gang, to finish the job. One way to avoid the Tackle is to go swimming. There are no Tackles in the Sea of Japan.

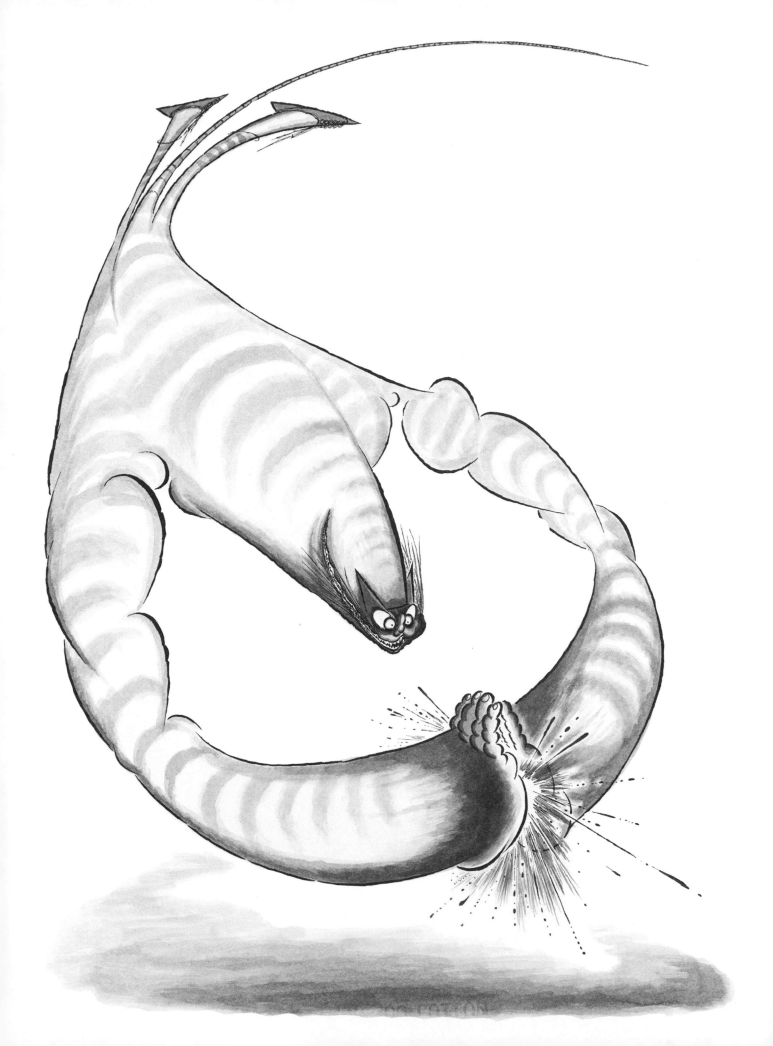

THE DIVOT

A rather flat, discouraged frog that frog fanciers and various do-gooders feel strongly should be replaced—that is, put back exactly on the spot from which he hopped in the first place. People feel very sanctimonious putting a Divot back; they feel they have done a good deed for the day. Sometimes they tamp the Divot down with shoes that have spikes on them as if to enforce the fact on the Divot that the Divot is to stay put. No one has ever *asked* the Divot if he or she wants to be "replaced." It may well be, after all, that the Divot would like to get to the nearest lake for a swim—a natural enough possibility for a frog—or perhaps even a-froggin' go . . . that is to say, join a little dance with the other Divots over there by the Casual Water. But the do-gooders will have none of this. They put up signs in the forest and meadows warning that DIVOTS MUST BE REPLACED—their assumption being that the Divot is very happy where he was.

THE PITCH

A rabbit of the Easter variety, white-furred, usually female, cuddly, red-ribboned, and desirable for taking to dances. Indeed, the gossip columns will announce as follows: "Carlton Fisk took the Pitch," or "Lee Mazzilli went with the Pitch." Or even, "Reggie Jackson reached for a Pitch on the corner." The Pitch never seems to escape attention, however hard she tries to escape the limelight. For example: "Pete Rose stroked a Pitch over the wall!" The Pitches are constantly being "looked over." Sometimes the Pitch gets riled up because of all this attention, thumps a long paw a few times against the dirt, and does something about it. In the columns the word appears: "George Brett was hit by the Pitch!" or, "A Pitch sent Rod Carew flying to the dirt!" or even, "A Pitch pinked Carl Yastrzemski in the ribs." Nonetheless the Pitch is a highly visible creature, much sought after and admired. "Here comes the Pitch!" is a breathless phrase that is uttered many hundreds of times, especially during the spring and summer months when the Pitches do not wear very much.

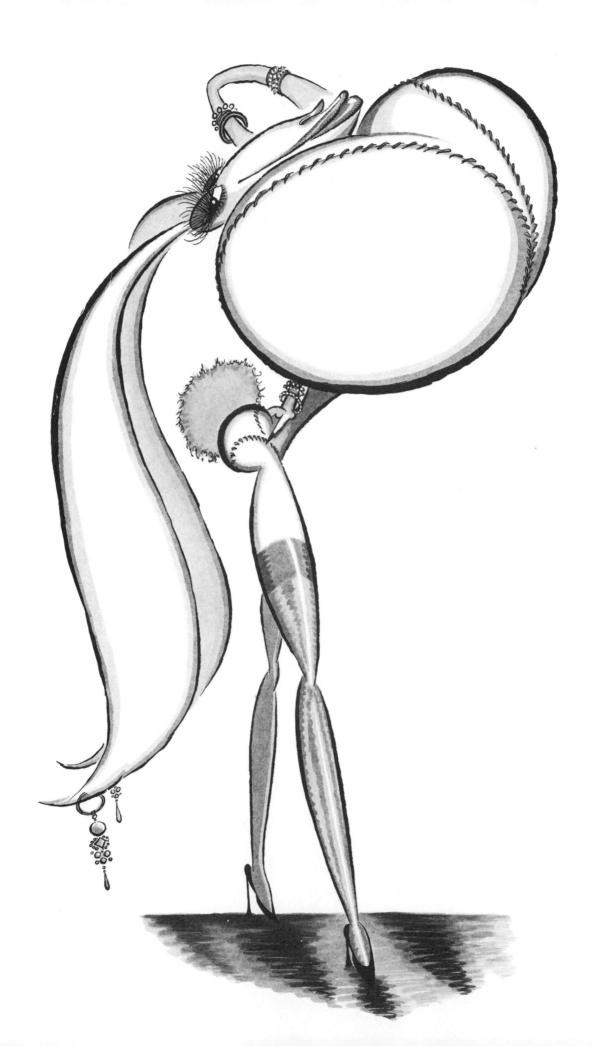

THE 24-SECOND CLOCK

A squat, box-shaped hedgehog with digital-red eyes that sits at the mouth of his burrow just off the corner of rectangular fields. He is rarely found anywhere else. Sometimes he is known as the Great Seiko, but there are other species, such as Longines. The animal has a curious cyclical habit—he inflates himself to the size of a small ox and then, with little second-long deflations of air, subsides to the size of a Ping-Pong ball, at which point he makes a loud buzzing sound and inflates with startling speed to his fullest size and begins the process anew. It takes him twenty-four seconds to do this. No one knows why he has picked this somewhat arbitrary figure of twenty-four. Finally, he winds down for the last time. He buzzes. He has, in the vernacular of those who study him, run out.

THE TWO-MINUTE WARNING

A ubiquitous and annoying member of the Jackdaw family who has learned to call out "Two minutes!" "Two minutes!" at unlikely moments—halfway into a bar examination, or in a plane 750 miles from Hawaii, or, suddenly, in the darkness of a lover's lane, or at an Adventist hillside doomsday meeting, or just as the curtain rises on the Third Act of Puccini's *La Bohème*. No one is quite sure who taught the Two-Minute Warning to give his dire announcement, or why he emits his cry in situations which cause great consternation and scurrying about. Even worse, the Warning never suggests what is going to happen at the conclusion of the two minutes. In fact, life seems to continue on as it did before. The Two-Minute Warning has a cousin known as the Three-Second Violation who frequents the rafters and flies down to bellow "Three seconds! Three seconds!" Neither is to be confused with the 24-Second Clock (cf).

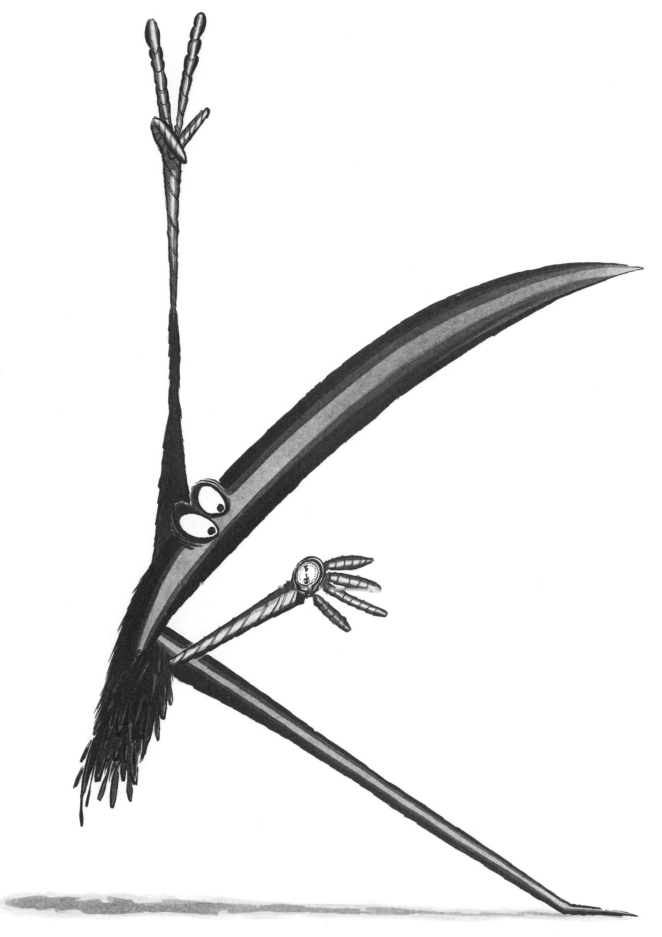

41

THE GIPPER

A small, stoatlike animal with large eyes, often brimming with tears, that lives in the back of clubhouse lockers, usually up on the top shelf with the Desenex foot powder and the tape rolls. He is often thought of as a team mascot. The Gipper has a curious hacking bark that sounds like the despairing cough of a consumptive. He sleeps with his eyes open and glazed, which tends to confuse people who assume that the Gipper is about to expire. Often his name is evoked in coaches' pregame and half-time pep talks on the mistaken assumption that a victory would cheer up the clubhouse Gipper. "Let's go out and win one for the Gipper!" is the way it is sometimes expressed. Often this sentiment is greeted by a low groan followed by a hacking cough from the Gipper himself, who does not like the champagne-guzzling, towel-snapping brouhaha of a victory celebration, and much prefers the quiet and gloom of a mind-boggling defeat.

43

THE INFIELD FLY RULE

Not many people, especially female, understand why there should be such a creature as the Infield Fly Rule. One wonders what his function is in the ecological scheme of things. Yet he continues to exist, lurking about the sedge grass, and on occasion the Infield Fly Rule is called out of the swamp to make sure he is still there. Calling for the Infield Fly Rule—like hog calling in Arkansas—is a peculiarly American activity.

What emerges is a heavy aquatic fowl that should stay out of the water but does not. The natural oils in his feathers do not keep him buoyant. The flapping and struggling sounds in the reeds at the edge of the pond in the twilight hours are usually the Infield Fly Rule trying to stay afloat. His bill is about all he manages to keep above the water. The reason he is called is often to see what the rest of him looks like.

"What is that mournful quacking?"
"They're calling the Infield Fly Rule."
"Why?"
"To see if he's there."

THE KICKING TEE

A bell-shaped animal that may or may not be a slope-shouldered groundhog, the Kicking Tee does not kick. He appears to have feet, but they are very small—just props to keep him from falling over. No one has seen the Tee kick so much as a pebble, or even scuff dust. Apparently, what the Tee enjoys doing most is to hoist an odd-shaped ball aloft on its shoulders, much like a girl holding up a beach ball on the seashore. The Kicking Tee does not get to enjoy this simple pastime for very long. Invariably, within seconds, the ball is violently removed from his grasp by an unseen force. One might suppose that the Kicking Tee would complain. But he does not. He is quite even-mannered. After a while he finds another ball to hold aloft until it is once again swept from his grasp. The Kicking Tee is usually up to this harmless activity on weekends. If you are terribly anxious to see one of these quite boring animals, he may be seen in a cold place named Green Bay, Wisconsin.

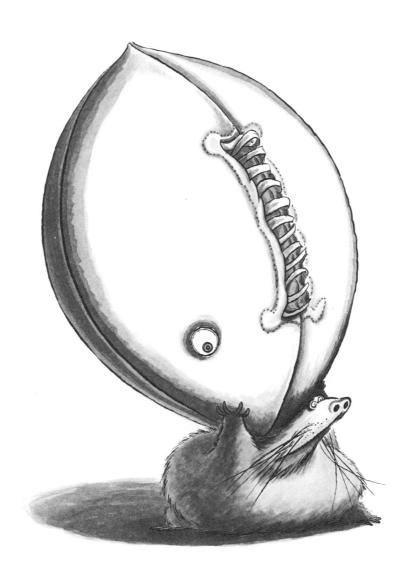

THE SCRUM

A large crustacean with many feet but no head that occasionally reminds those who are unfortunate enough to come upon him of an enormous, tailless barnacle-backed horseshoe crab. He is active on large fields or "pitches," covering the ground in random confusion. The Scrum is inevitably attended in an apparent symbiotic relationship by a curious, nervous, crablike companion known as the Fly Half, who for obscure reasons spends his life trying to drop an oval pebble under the carapace of the Scrum in amongst his myriad of feet. The Scrum becomes very agitated when the pebble is thrust underneath him. He scrabbles around trying to kick the pebble out. Sometimes he literally collapses in his efforts. Observers cry out, "My God, the Scrum over there has collapsed!" Anyone venturing near the Scrum when he is active would be aware of the creature's stomach being in an uproar—gasps, sharp cries, yelps of pain, gurgles of effort. Clouds of sweat rise from the animal steamily. The Scrum, in short, is definitely not an individual one would want to invite in for tea.

THE JUNKBALL

A kindly member of the falcon family, the Junkball seems equipped to catch rabbits—that is to say, in conformation he looks very similar to other members of his species, such as the dreaded Slider or the bellicose Knuckler or the nefarious Hummer. He looks as though it would be easy for him to swerve sharply in sudden flight, or flutter and dive, or change pace, or simply emit a large cry as he swoops on a rabbit. But he does none of these things. He floats out with a sweet benign smile. Even a rabbit or so has been known to reach up and take a disdainful poke at him. The Junkball flies on to his leather hollow. Birds of ingrained habit, Junkballs fly sixty feet four inches, exactly, from one leather hollow to another leather hollow. They land with a small pop! They are not interested in rabbits at all.

THE TWI-NIGHT DOUBLEHEADER

This is what causes many a child to burst into tears when his father says he is going off to one. The child imagines something along the lines of a volcano-sized hydra. In fact, the Twi-Night Doubleheader is hardly anything to get riled up about—being a small cinch worm. The worm sometimes makes a loop or so forward, and then often backwards, so that to the imaginative observer the creature appears to have two heads. He emerges in the evening, most usually in the months of August and September. Heavy rains in the summer are apparently instrumental in the Twi-Night Doubleheader's appearance later on. Sometimes the Twi-Night Doubleheader is "split"—that is to say, the worm is divided by people interested to see if both ends work independent of each other. They do. Being split is of small consequence to the Twi-Night Doubleheader since the creature is extremely primitive and gets along perfectly well whether split or not. Obviously those who go to see Twi-Night Doubleheaders have nothing better to do with their evenings.

THE STUFF

The Stuff is a peculiar beast that would like to be a head on the wall of a sportsman's den. The Stuff imagines himself up there next to the kudu head peering down on the press of a cocktail party to listen in on conversations. Occasionally, the Stuff protrudes the front end of his body through the bead curtain hanging in front of a den door and *pretends* to be stuffed. Often he gets away with it. He is an impressive animal, at least the front end of him—a horn, a tusk, an antler, and a big lip, the sort of excessive head that would indeed grace the wall of a den . . . at least in Fort Worth, Texas. The sight of the Stuff is enough to get people to exclaim in wonder. Naturally, the Stuff is very pleased at the attention. Sometimes, however, he rolls his eyes at something overheard in the conversation below and he is discovered. Consternation! The host is called. He is outraged. The Stuff is "rejected," which is the worst thing that can happen to the Stuff.

THE ATHLETE'S FOOT

A very determined member of the snail family that creeps along on his foot dreaming about being the heavyweight champion of the world. Some authorities say that the Athlete's Foot has a very nifty left hook to throw, but in truth no one has seen it. If he throws anything it would have to be that big foot of his. *That* he does have—a truly substantial foot.

A midge, one of the smaller variety, known as the Athletic Supporter, constantly follows the Athlete's Foot around. He is convinced that the Foot will indeed win the heavyweight championship of the world. He says the Foot is the "Greatest." He carries a little stool for the Foot to sit on in his corner. He has a towel with which to fan the Foot, and a bucket for the Foot to spit in.

THE SACRIFICE FLY

As the name suggests, the Sacrifice Fly is a fly who makes great personal sacrifices. As flies go, he is lean, long-limbed, and would be considered good-looking if he were not so giving of himself—a habit that has left him looking rather shopworn. He has a right arm which he is always giving away and also a left leg. He skins out of the shirts on his back and gives them to those he feels (often mistakenly) are less fortunate than himself. He gives advances to friends. He can always be relied on for a handout to get people home. He is spoken of kindly: "The Sacrifice Fly got Jones home." With a little more effort on his part, and perhaps a little luck, he could very easily become a Two-Bagger (cf) or even a Round Tripper (cf), but he prefers to be giving of himself. Sometimes he has only one leg left to stand on. His flight is ungainly. He twists high in the sky. He glints in the sun. People snap down their sunglasses and stare up at him.

THE TWO-BAGGER

Not to be confused with a One-Bagger, which has one, or a Three-Bagger, which has three. The Two-Bagger has two. Most authorities prefer the Two-Bagger to the One-Bagger. He often raises his spikes as he slants down and lands on his perch. He fluffs his feathers and dusts himself off. A piece of tobacco works in the corner of his beak. He is apparently very pleased to be where he is. But in fact he is only temporarily satisfied. A nomadic restless sort, he must move on. Some authorities believe he wishes to go and sit in the shade of a dugout in the reeds. He does a lot of "inching off," flying out a few yards into the lonely spaces where his enemies, including the Perfectly Executed Pickoff, wait for him. Sometimes he dies while inching off. The Two-Bagger exemplifies great success followed by a lot of worry.

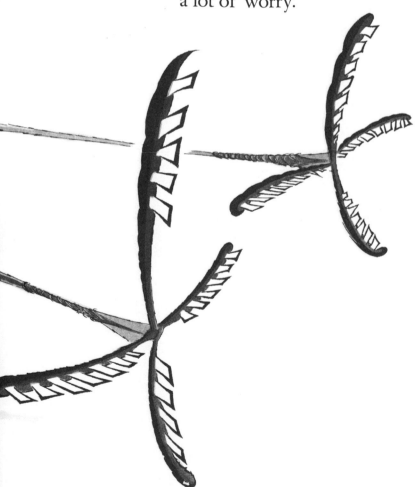

THE ROUND TRIPPER

A Sacrifice Fly (cf) that on occasion goes completely off his rocker and changes character violently. Usually, there is great rejoicing at this transformation, since the Sacrifice Fly is such a dolt that it is heartwarming to see him involved in excessive behavior. The Round Tripper is occasionally called the Ruthian Blast, named after George Herman (Babe) Ruth, a Sacrifice Fly from Baltimore, Maryland, who exemplified the wilder aspects of the species. The transformation from the state of being a Sacrifice Fly to that of a Round Tripper is compared by many to what happens to the werewolf at the first ray of the moon. He becomes pin-striped. Turnip-shaped. Candy bars are named after him. He likes to point into the distance and go there. He enjoys flying over fences and walls to see what is on the other side. He likes to drop into seats.

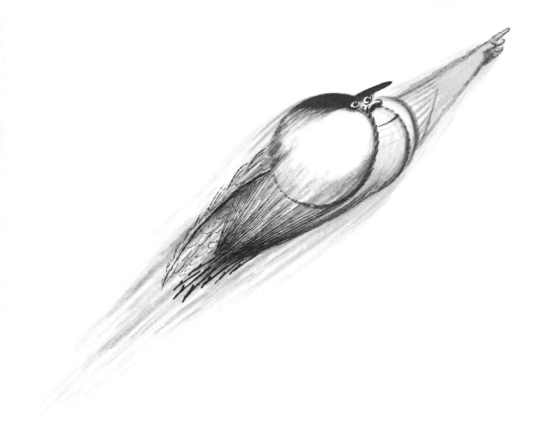

63

THE SAFETY

The Safety is a pint-sized giraffe who hopes something will come his way. He can be spotted standing very much by himself in a field, pacing around, occasionally giving a little hop to see if anyone is turning up. When the Tight End or the Wide Receiver is loose on the veldt, he rushes over as if to embrace him. He is especially enamored of a flying creature known as the Bomb. He reaches for her. He fights the Tight End and the Wide Receiver for the affection of the Bomb. Some think that the Safety, as well as others, are somewhat daffy in this respect, since the Bomb is rather plain, ovoid, and has only one set of laces. Her flight is measured in yards rather than miles, and when the Bomb lands she first bobbles around erratically and then rocks back and forth before settling into a motionless sulk in the grass.

THE KILLER INSTINCT

A caged canary of great value and social significance. To lack a Killer Instinct is to fess up to moral sloth and Not Trying to Keep Up with the Joneses. No one likes to admit to not having a Killer Instinct any more than one would confess to not having a second car in the garage or a Sense of Humor, which is a distant parakeetlike cousin of the Killer Instinct. Unhappily, the Killer Instinct is not on sale in pet shops. The bird is passed down from one generation to another—as if a genetic gift. Sometimes a coach will install a Killer Instinct in the home of one of his charges, but most people are born with the bird right there waiting in the delivery room. Jack Dempsey had a lot of Killer Instincts. Floyd Patterson may have had one, but he kept the creature out in the back somewhere.

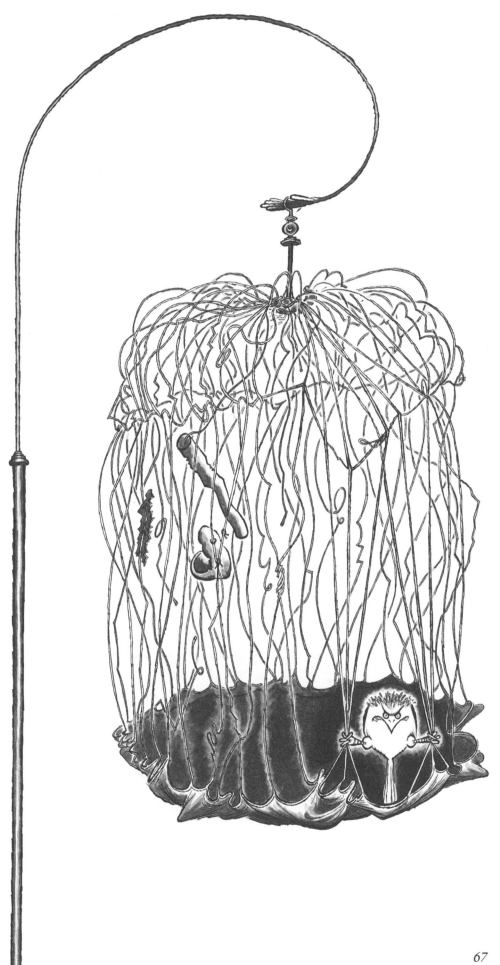

THE WHIFF

The Whiff is a gregarious but unhappy finch who would like to make social contact with other species such as the Slider, the Knuckler, or the Hummer. The Whiff sits on a branch close by a flyway where they flash by on the hunt in the evening and he calls to them to stop and chat. No one is impressed. Nobody stops. The Whiff looks down the lane of trees for the next arrival. The Whiff is most common in parks and glades frequented by these predators along with others such as the Drop, and the Screwball. On occasion the Whiff is found on the meadows with the Casual Water, the Mashie, the Cleek, the Duck Hook, and the Waggle. In these surroundings the Whiff is considered very bad news indeed, and anyone associated with him is advised to leave the area and take up something else quickly.

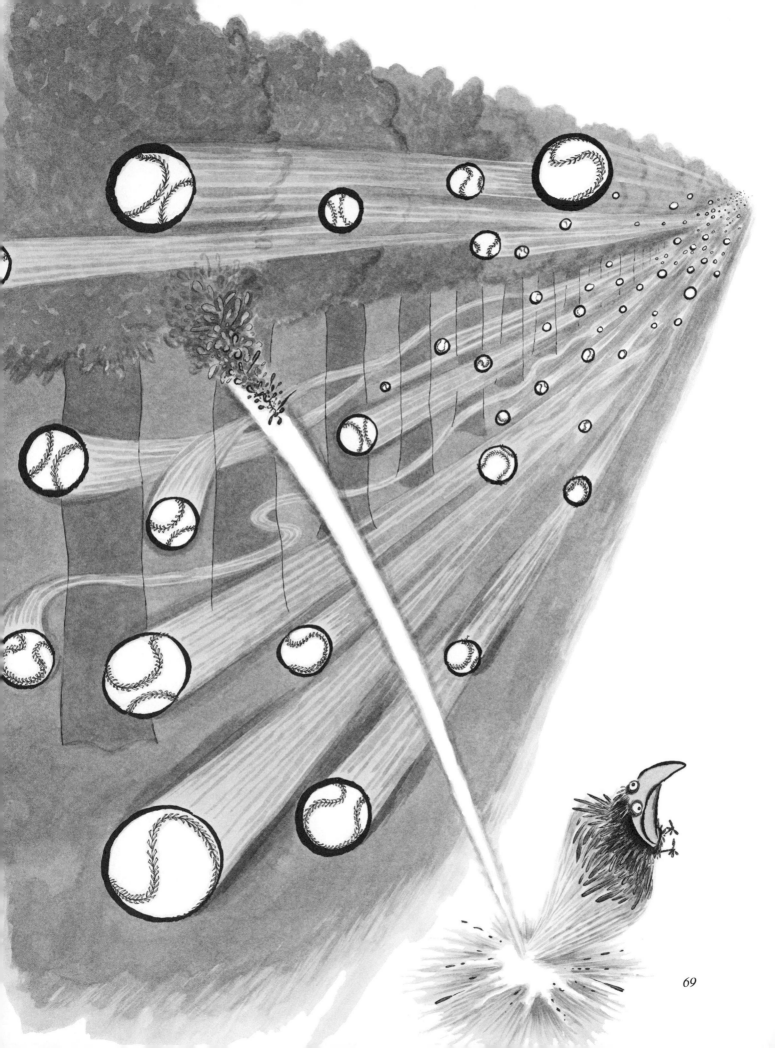

THE NAT'L ANTHEM

A distant relative of the Seventh Inning Stretch, although invariably the Nat'l Anthem appears earlier in the afternoon. It is a large morpho butterfly. Everybody stands up and cranes to see it. Hats are removed. The Nat'l Anthem has the reputation of depositing its eggs between the hatband and the felt, and while people revere the Nat'l Anthem, they like their hats. So people stand straight and quietly, hoping that the Nat'l Anthem will not notice their hats as it flutters by. Military people, who are bound by regulations to keep their hats on, hold their right hands at the ready to snap at the Nat'l Anthem should it sweep down on them. The genus of the Nat'l Anthem is large, and for some odd reason numbers exactly the complement of the General Assembly of the United Nations. Some Nat'l Anthems are colorful and brassy; others are drab. The Romanians have a Nat'l Anthem that is of no interest at all. Some are rarely identifiable outside their country of origin. Very few people would be able to recognize the Sudanese Nat'l Anthem if it flew by. On the other hand, everyone knows the French variety, with its vivid tricolor wing pattern. Nat'l Anthems, whatever their nationality, are somehow attracted by very large crowds. If you want to see a Nat'l Anthem, don't bother standing alone in a field.

THE BIG LEAGUE SCOUT

A heavily paunched bird who was once a cardinal, or a bluejay, or an oriole, or even a mud hen of Toledo, but is now grizzled and quite unfit to do what he did in his prime. He sits heavily on the edge of the green fields in the early spring and watches younger and trimmer versions of himself with great wrists which can hit the long ball. They too will one day become Big League Scouts unless they learn banking in the meantime. It is a progression as inevitable as the changing of the seasons. The Big League Scout dreams of some day becoming a Big League Manager—a more heavily paunched and plumaged creature on the evolutionary scale—but the fancy is idle since there are only twenty-six Big League Managers, who utilize twenty-six coveted roosting sites. They may leave a roosting site but only to trade one with another Big League Manager. Big League Scouts ride in the back of buses because their wings are tired.

THE FIELDING GEM

A vegetable, short on leaves, but with bright red berries, that insists on wearing a tuxedo and trying to crash deb parties at the Sherry Netherlands. The Fielding Gem gets away with it. It looks very snappy, and those who spot it are often incredulous: "Wasn't that a Fielding Gem? Whew!" The Fielding Gem is rarely described as such verbally. One might *write* about it in a diary ("Saw a Fielding Gem today"), but one would not tend to turn to one's neighbor and announce, "Look! A Fielding Gem!" What is more likely to happen when a Fielding Gem turns up in the lobby of the Sherry Netherlands, say, is that a Holy Cow! (cf) will emerge from the gunk of a potted palm.

THE HOLY COW!

A newt, he trails an exclamation point after him as he emerges from the gunk. He has low cheekbones. A creature of curious habit, he inevitably materializes at occasions of great moment—when the Round Tripper (cf) has put in an appearance, or the Fielding Gem (cf), or when the Stuff (cf) is rejected. *This* is the time for the Holy Cow! He almost never emerges at the sight of a Two-Bagger (cf). The Two-Bagger does not excite the Holy Cow! Neither does the Junkball (cf).

THE FLEA-FLICKER

A long-fingered gibbon who gets his kicks from flicking fleas—an unfortunate preoccupation since he has no fleas of his own to flick. So he must flick the fleas off other animals, very often, victimizing the Safety (cf) or the Cornerback. The Flea-Flicker is a rare animal and puts in a surprise appearance only once or twice a year, invariably in the late autumn months. Usually the Flea-Flicker appears at times of the most dire situations—during violent thunderstorms; earthshakings; blights of the Dutch Elm Disease; the darkening of the sun by coots; a proliferation of sea urchins riding in on the surf . . . times, in short, that try men's souls. It seems almost an impertinence that this strange animal should appear at such desperate moments with this ridiculous absorbing concern to flick fleas. But that is what he wants to do—what more can one say?

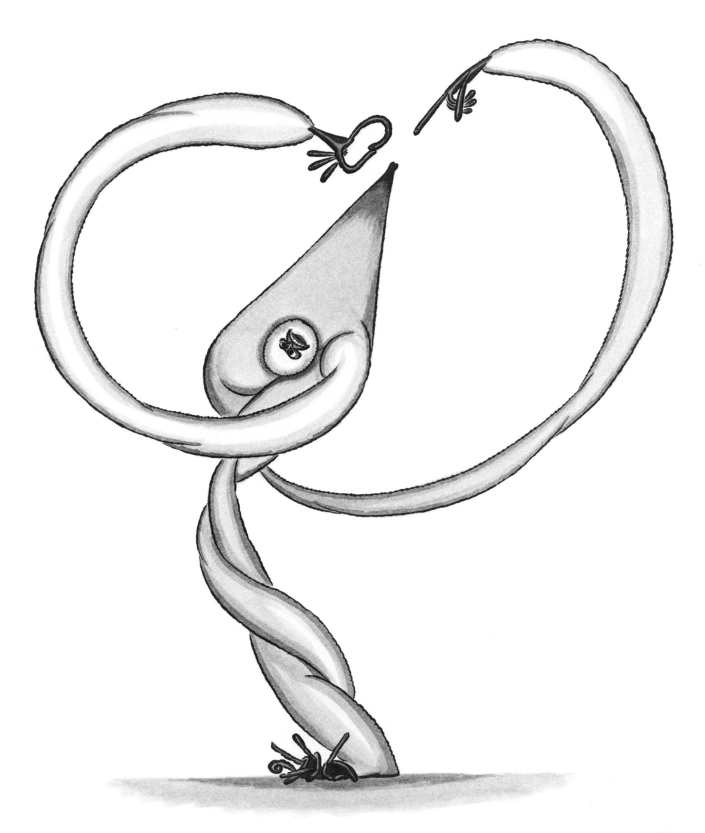

THE BUSTED FLUSH

A handsome-looking, rather foppish member of the oriole family famous for his vocal inability to complete an ascending scale of five musical notes in proper order. He will sing, C, D, E, F, with mounting excitement as he hopes for the perfect ultimate! But what emerges from his pulsating throat is a B-flat, or a nontonal belch, or, on occasion, the cannon fusillade from Tchaikovsky's *1812 Overture*. Sometimes the Busted Flush tries to fake his way through the exercise. Finally, his exasperated cronies call on him to produce or shut up. He starts. C, D, E, F float nicely into the evening air, but then he fails miserably on the last note. On the surrounding branches his cronies chuckle cruelly because they know he has gone bust yet again.

THE SUICIDE SQUEEZE

A rather depressing misanthropic creature of indeterminate origins—but with some serpent in him, and perhaps a bit of hedgehog—who on rare occasions tries to do away with himself . . . usually by pressing into corners or wrapping himself around himself. Not surprisingly, the Suicide Squeeze rarely succeeds. There is inevitably great rejoicing and cries of admiration when he *does* succeed—which would suggest the lack of popularity of this animal. Many authorities wish he would try it more often.

THE SERVICE BREAK

A torpedolike fish which resembles the Wahoo. It is not widely distributed. There are very few Service Breaks in the lakes of Uganda. In recent times these fish (*Bjornus Borgus*) have been found in the waters off Sweden. For many years the Australian reefs had a great many Service Breaks and traditionally the California coast has been an excellent spawning ground. The Service Break is invariably preceded by a small pilot fish called the Break Point. "Here's a Break Point," the fisherman will observe, looking for the long, snoutish forequarters of the Service Break following along behind. The Break Point is more common than the Service Break. In fact no one has ever seen a Service Break not preceded by a Break Point, though it is possible to sight a Break Point without a Service Break. Fishermen complain, "Well, we've had six Break Points so far and not one Service Break."

THE TECHNICAL FOUL

The Technical Foul is not a fowl, as one might suppose, and has nothing to do with the Foul Tip (cf). The Foul is a member of the canine family, usually kept on a leash by law enforcement officers and used on patrol in such depressed areas as the gardens of Boston and Madison Square. The Foul is not much of a deterrent on his own. The usual practice is to pick him up by the tail, whirl him around in the circular motion of the hammer thrower, and then step forward and slap the miscreant across the face. To be "slapped" or "hit" with a Technical Foul is not a pleasant experience for any of the principals involved. The officer who does the slapping is usually apoplectic with rage at having been forced to bestow the Technical, and probably exhausted from the labor involved in whirling the beast around; the person slapped with the Technical Foul usually becomes quite morose, rarely contrite, and he sulks moodily by a water cooler. Sometimes he gets slapped *twice* with a Technical Foul and that means he must flee into the deepest recesses of the gardens to sulk. Nobody has ever asked the Technical Foul what it is like to be picked up by the tail and used as an implement, but it cannot be much fun.

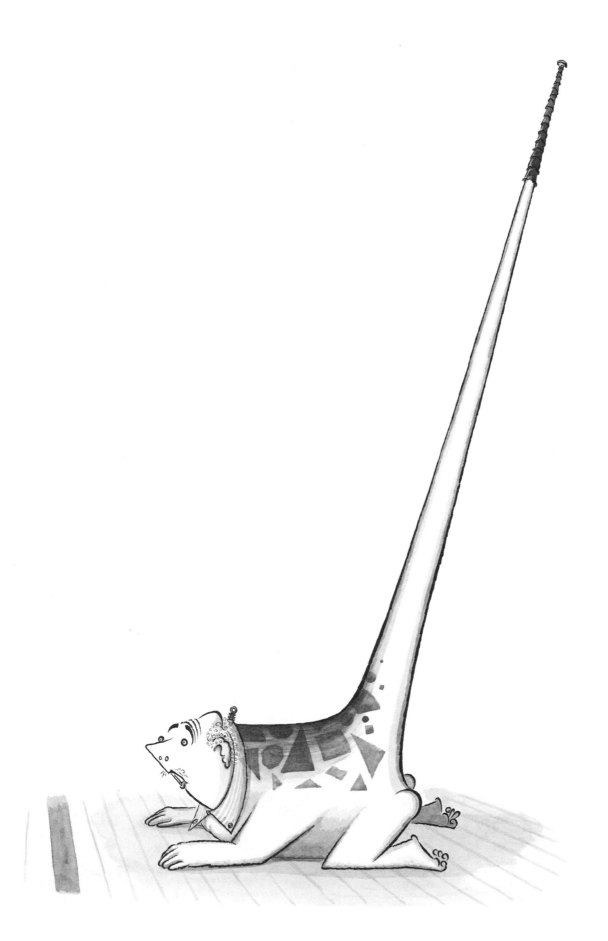

THE GOOD WOOD

A curious, very stiff-jointed, clumsy, chunky-bodied bird, not unlike a stout eagle—known for its propensity for perching on orbs. The trouble is that the Good Wood has trouble landing on orbs. He tends to alight at such a speed that he topples and falls off forward. But the Good Wood is an appealing bird; people do not mind picking him up and setting him carefully on the nearest orb. For those Samaritans who have helped the Good Wood there is always the pleasure of mentioning their deed to friends: "Yesterday, I got the Good Wood on the ball." The Good Wood has a close cousin, the Point, which rather than perching on orbs prefers the edge of boards. He is not adept at this either. He is assisted, much as the Good Wood is, by helpful citizens who put him up on the board. The Point travels in tightly knit flocks, so that one tends to speak of putting Points on the board, rather than a single Point. It is a compulsive habit—putting Points on the board. People explain, "It's just a matter of putting some Points on the board."

THE FOUL TIP

The Foul Tip is a variety of hawk moth with a strange predilection for trying to sniff leather, invariably in the pocket of a glove on someone's hand. Why the Foul Tip isn't satisfied with scenting the leather of a car seat, or the thong of a sandal, or just settling into the palm of a glove lying out on the grass, no one knows. Authorities believe that the warmth and the slight exudate of linseed oil may have something to do with this peculiar attraction. There are many other varieties of Foul (thank goodness!)—the Pop, the High Twister, the Loud; there is a common species which likes to "fly back over the roof"; there is also the Foul Pole, a shy, thin, rather aloof specimen. The demeanor of Fouls varies. Some are known to "scream." There is one variety that attacks the shod foot, apparently wishing to bite into the shoe leather. The Foul Tip is by no means as voracious. He is satisfied simply to dart in and out of a glove—much like a hummingbird sampling a flower's nectar.

THE BALK

The Balk is a seldom-seen member of the woodchuck species that lives under a circular bare mound on which there is a small cheesecloth bag filled for some reason with rosin. Some authorities believe that Balks are nocturnal and come out in the predawn hours to play a kind of tossing game with the rosin bag. In any case, when the Balk is spotted, there is almost always a rosin bag nearby. Some think the Balk is beguiling. He is called for on occasion: "Balk! Balk!" But he rarely appears. When he does, there is invariably a great deal of discussion whether it actually was or was not a Balk that was seen. The Balk is not a substantial animal. He does not rear out of his burrow and do something odd with the rosin bag that would be interesting. He is a skulker, and very retiring. The tip of an ear appears. Was it or was it not a Balk? Shouts go up, "Balk! Balk!" Who knows? To hell with the Balk.

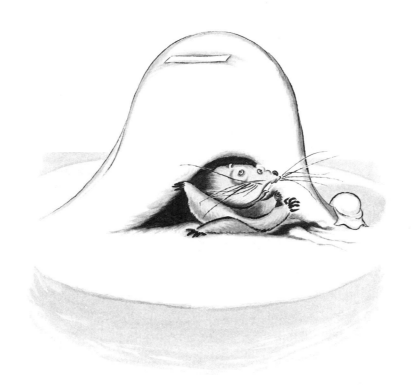

THE NOSE GUARD

The Nose Guard is a youngish moose who likes to get very close to people. He poises above them. Nobody knows why the Nose Guard is on the forward edge of the doorsill when one opens the door to leave for work, or why the animal tends to loom over one during the weeding of the lawn. Some authorities believe that the Nose Guard's manner is intimidating because he would rather be a natural phenomenon such as a thunderstorm or a tidal wave. A more likely solution is that the Nose Guard wishes to be close to others in order to embrace them spontaneously. A gregarious sort (many Nose Guards belong to the Yale Club), the Nose Guard is invariably in the center of things and is often to be found in the vicinity of Defensive Huddles. There are many who do not enjoy being embraced by a Nose Guard. A scream is too often the result.

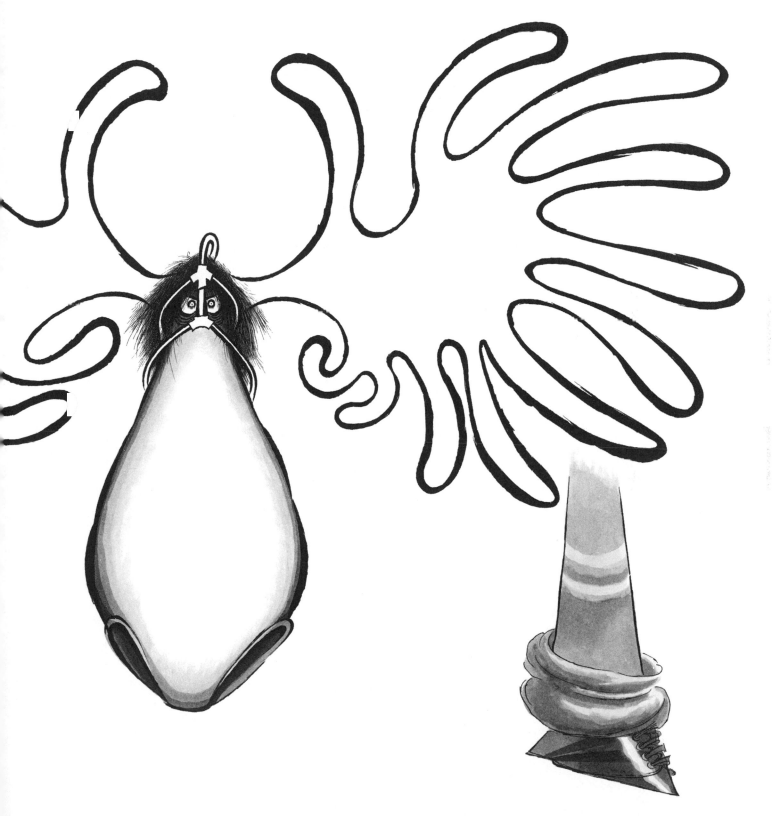

THE PUCK

A nonedible root. There are those who try to eat the Puck, often at considerable damage to their teeth. A great many people confuse the Puck with a truffle and mistakenly try to harvest it with a great deal of enthusiasm. Indeed, the Puck is fought over with such vigor in dark corners that a kind of harvesting ritual has evolved. The farmers collect in a circle and peer down at a symbolic Puck in a short ceremony known as the Face-off. But then venality gets the best of everyone and a struggle breaks out over this worthless root. A practical solution would be to find some way of cooking the Puck so that it was halfway palatable. At least, that would make all the fussing over the Puck worthwhile. Another inedible root that causes a great deal of strife and heaving is the Pigskin, larger than the Puck, but not so large as a watermelon, whose shape it resembles and which is slightly more pliable and toothsome—but not much. Actually, more farmers struggle over the Pigskin than the Puck, with as many as twenty-two men at a time clawing and biting, and even stiff-arming, to call it their own.

THE INTENTIONAL WALK

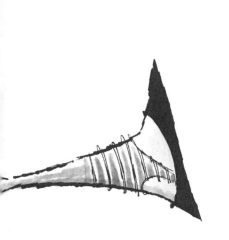

A chickadee-like fowl about the size of a Great Dane. Not to be confused with its close relative the Unintentional Walk. The Intentional is suave, intelligent, clean-toed, and has been known to sport a small flower. His nest is in order. He is a product of family planning. The Unintentional, on the other hand, is very likely the result of an illicit union—perhaps the responsibility of such shady characters as the Way-Outside, the In-the-Dirt, the Pitchout, and the absolutely disgraceful All-the-Way-Back-to-the-Screen. The Unintentionals are bad news. Even one Unintentional can "hurt you," but two is worse, and three at the same time is really asking for it. That is not to suggest that his cousin, the Intentional Walk, is always what you hope for. He can turn as sour as the Unintentional and hurt you just as much. Sometimes the best thing, regarding these Walks, is to stay in a dugout and hope for rain.

THE FINAL SCORE

A minute species of silverfish which lives in
the bindings of record books and in the dust of
old newspaper stacks. He is not much to look at,
frankly, but he has a tremendously inflated
reputation. Some authorities even say that in the
scheme of things the Final Score is "all that
matters"; others think that may be putting it too
boldly. After all, only about half the people who
get to see the Final Score really approve. The
others are disappointed. If the Final Score is a
variety known as the Tie, all the people who have
seen him go home and start kissing their sisters.
The fact remains that the Final Score ends up in
the records of the past. He is there to be relished
or mourned over, depending upon how a person
feels about these strange creatures. There may be
one in this book. Slap the covers open and shut to see.

ABOUT THE AUTHOR AND ARTIST

George Plimpton is the editor of the literary quarterly *The Paris Review*. He is the author of a number of books, most of them with a sports background: *Out of My League, Paper Lion, The Bogey Man, Mad Ducks and Bears, One More July, Shadow Box*, and others. He is the co-author with Jean Stein of *American Journey: The Times of Robert F. Kennedy*, and *Edie, An American Biography*; and he is the editor of the five-volume series *Writers at Work*, interviews on the craft of writing from the *Paris Review*.

Arnold Roth is a free-lance cartoonist who illustrates for many magazines, among which are *Sports Illustrated, Inside Sports, TV Guide*, and *Esquire*. He does a monthly feature about America for *Punch* magazine in London. Mr. Roth has illustrated many books, including four books for children which dealt with puzzles, science, sports, and pets. Born, raised, and educated in Philadelphia, Pennsylvania, Mr. Roth lives in Princeton, New Jersey, where he sometimes plays the saxophone for relaxation and neighborhood disharmony. Mr. Roth is a baseball nut.